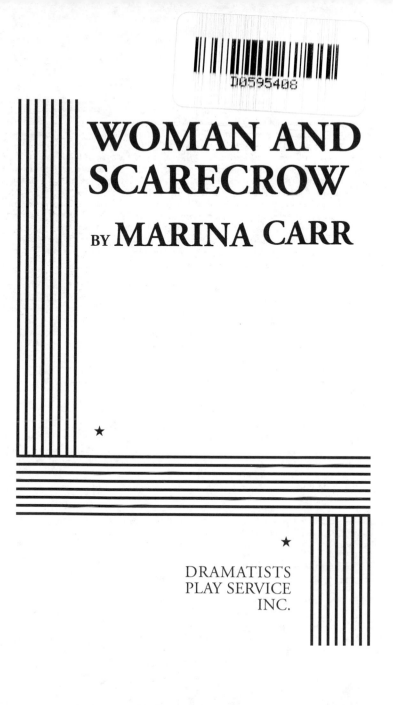

WOMAN AND SCARECROW

BY **MARINA CARR**

★

★

DRAMATISTS
PLAY SERVICE
INC.

WOMAN AND SCARECROW
Copyright © 2010, Marina Carr

All Rights Reserved

SPECIAL NOTE
Anyone receiving permission to produce WOMAN AND SCARECROW is required to give credit to the Author as sole and exclusive Author of the Play on the title page of all programs distributed in connection with performances of the Play and in all instances in which the title of the Play appears for purposes of advertising, publicizing or otherwise exploiting the Play and/or a production thereof. The name of the Author must appear on a separate line, in which no other name appears, immediately beneath the title and in size of type equal to 50% of the size of the largest, most prominent letter used for the title of the Play. No person, firm or entity may receive credit larger or more prominent than that accorded the Author. The following acknowledgment must appear on the title page in all programs distributed in connection with performances of the Play:

WOMAN AND SCARECROW was first performed on June 16, 2006
at the Royal Court Jerwood Theatre Upstairs, Sloane Square, London.

SPECIAL NOTE ON SONGS AND RECORDINGS
For performances of copyrighted songs, arrangements or recordings mentioned in this Play, the permission of the copyright owner(s) must be obtained. Other songs, arrangements or recordings may be substituted provided permission from the copyright owner(s) of such songs, arrangements or recordings is obtained; or songs, arrangements or recordings in the public domain may be substituted.

WOMAN AND SCARECROW received its world premiere at the Royal Court Theatre in London, England, on June 16, 2006. It was directed by Ramin Gray; the production design was by Lizzie Clachan; and the sound design was by Emma Laxton. The cast was as follows:

WOMAN .... Fiona Shaw
SCARECROW .... Brid Brennan
HIM .... Peter Gowen
AUNTIE AH .... Stella McCusker

WOMAN AND SCARECROW received its American premiere by the Mead Theatre Lab, in Washington, D.C., on May 7, 2009. It was directed by Des Kennedy; the set and costume designs were by Lynly Saunders; the lighting design was by Marianne Meadows; and the sound design was by David Crandall. The cast was as follows:

WOMAN .... Jennifer Mendenhall
SCARECROW .... Nanna Ingvarsson
HIM .... Brian Hemmingsen
AUNTIE AH .... Rena Cherry Brown

CHARACTERS

WOMAN

SCARECROW

HIM

AUNTIE AH

SET

A bed. A wardrobe. A CD player.

TIME

The present.

WOMAN AND SCARECROW

ACT ONE

Woman lies in the bed gaunt and ill. Scarecrow stands beside her.

WOMAN. I ran west to die.

SCARECROW. You ran south, and you didn't run, you crawled.

WOMAN. I ran west. West! Why would I go south?

SCARECROW. You got lost.

WOMAN. I thought you were the navigator.

SCARECROW. They found you under a bronze statue of a man with his arm pointing out to sea.

WOMAN. Did they? ... Oh yeah, and his eyes fixed beyond the horizon and I remember thinking before I passed out, if I can't see the horizon myself, at least I'm near something that can. Why didn't you help me get back west?

SCARECROW. We're not cowboys.

WOMAN. I started out west. I'd like to finish there.

SCARECROW. When you could have gone west, you refused.

WOMAN. No, listen to me. If I could get across the Shannon once more, maybe the air would perform some sort of miracle ... I might live.

SCARECROW. You think crossing the Shannon is all it takes?

WOMAN. What you asked was impossible at the time.

SCARECROW. I would've looked after you. The world would have looked after you. I was getting used to it here. I was just settling in and now you're going to cart me off with you.

WOMAN. Suppose we headed west again. Just got up and walked.

SCARECROW. Walking is no longer an option. He's waiting in the wardrobe. Can't you hear him sucking his oily black wings?

WOMAN. In the wardrobe? In my wardrobe?

SCARECROW. He moved in while you were away. Do you want to see him?

WOMAN. No! Good God, no. Tell him to go away. *(Scarecrow goes to wardrobe, opens door.)*

SCARECROW. Go away … please. *(Sound of a muffled laugh from the wardrobe. A deep-throated guffaw.)* Yes, I understand this is all in a day's work for you, but this is her wardrobe and she requests your departure from it. *(Muffled glottal sounds from the wardrobe.)* I know, but she requests your departure from her wardrobe. *(An angry low outburst of growls and consonants. Scarecrow backs away, closes the door timidly.)*

WOMAN. Is he gone?

SCARECROW. Of course he's not gone, and don't annoy him anymore or he'll take you right now.

WOMAN. But I'm not ready.

SCARECROW. You think all the dead were ready? That thing will eat you alive. He doesn't care. I've seen him in action. He's in there now, making a bracelet out of infant anklet bones.

WOMAN. He's taken enough of mine before their time. I thought my tribe were due a break.

SCARECROW. It seems not.

WOMAN. Put on some music to drown him out.

SCARECROW. What do you want to hear?

WOMAN. Demis Roussos.

SCARECROW. No way. Not again.

WOMAN. Just do as I say.

SCARECROW. All my life I've been doing as you say and look where it's landed us.

WOMAN. And what exactly are your objections to Demis Roussos?

SCARECROW. Where to start?

WOMAN. He's sentimental I know, and the dentist on the 28th. Who will remember that? Put on the music. I'm asking you nicely. I'm asking you nicely. If you don't put him on, I'll … I'll …

SCARECROW. You'll what … if I don't put him on you'll do what?

WOMAN. I'll stop breathing this second.

SCARECROW. Go on! Stop! Let me see you stop breathing. Remember him in there. Go on! Stop!

WOMAN. I'm not playing with you. I'm going to count to three. If by three I don't hear "My Friend the Wind" blasting off the CD I'm going to put an end to it all. One. Two. Three. *(Scarecrow stands there defiantly.)* Right. That's it. Goodbye, you vicious parasite that's led me a crazy dance. Barking orders to kingdom come. All that unnecessary guilt! All those sly commands! All that wrong advice! All that metaphysical claptrap! Goodbye and good riddance, you stinking old turkey box. *(Woman stops breathing. Things are calm for a while as they eyeball one another. Then both start to go red in the face. Then Woman starts thrashing around, Scarecrow clutches her throat, doubled over, they both fight it a while, refusing to give in. Eventually Scarecrow reels towards CD player and struggles to put on music. Woman inhales violently as soon as she hears music, Scarecrow falls to the floor panting. They come to slowly as a song like Demis Roussos belting out "My Friend the Wind" or "Forever and Ever" plays … Woman croons along softly, raising a hand and conducting the proceedings.*)* Now that's all I wanted … I spoke to a chef once at a party, what was his name … anyway, it turned out he had cooked for Demis Roussos. The man ate six lobsters in one sitting. Now that's what I call passion for living. A man who can eat six lobsters, well, there's no stopping him. *(Silence from Scarecrow, who lies on the ground fuming.)* Is there? *(Silence.)* Thick are we? Thick as a brick. I warned you.

SCARECROW. You nearly took us to the blue beyond.

WOMAN. Now you know who's boss. I love this. This is great. Gets me churning. *(Shouts over the music.)* I was meant for someone of Demis Roussos' magnitude. Someone who can devour six lobsters as an appetiser. You can hear the lobsters in his voice. Floor of the sea stuff. Greek sea stuff written off by snobs like you.

SCARECROW. This has been your problem all along.

WOMAN. *(Shouts over the music.)* What?

SCARECROW. All this gush. All this hugeness.

WOMAN. Speak up!

SCARECROW. *(Shouts over the music.)* All these passions and nothing, nothing back of them.

WOMAN. So I'm not cold and articulate like you. I have no reserve. No restraint. No, what do they call that awful quality they rate so highly these days?

---

* See Special Note on Songs and Recordings on copyright page.

SCARECROW. Subtlety?

WOMAN. Yes, I have none of that. What else do I lack>?

SCARECROW. An eternal sense.

WOMAN. That's right. I can't even see tomorrow.

SCARECROW. There'll hardly be one now

WOMAN. Oh the children … the children.

SCARECROW. This is more of it. If you'd just shut up for five seconds about your children. All those pregnancies, how many was it, forty-four, all …

WOMAN. It was eight. Eight. Nine if you count the one who didn't make it. My little half-moon baby with the shock of blond hair. Where are you now, my half-cooked thing? Why couldn't you bear me? Why couldn't you stay the course? Did something sift into the womb that appalled you? I should've had nine. There should've been nine in the photograph. Oh my God, I'm not over him yet … I'll never be over his … what … his what? You're the articulate one … his what?

SCARECROW. That he came and went so quickly.

WOMAN. Gone before he was here.

SCARECROW. Did it ever occur to you that he was a signal?

WOMAN. A signal of what?

SCARECROW. A pointer to this.

WOMAN. Leave my children out of the witch turnings of your mind.

SCARECROW. Numbers. You just wanted numbers. You just wanted to look and say, this one is mine, and this one and this and him and her and all those and that pair up there in the oak tree. Mine. All mine. That's what you wanted. Greedy for numbers. Insatiable for the head count. The leg count. I own sixteen pairs of legs and the two that didn't make it and eight noses and sixteen eyes and the two that didn't make it and sixteen ears and eighty fingers and eighty toes and reciting their names and ages to knock yourself out after another exhausting day of counting and coveting and even still wondering if you could squeeze another one in as you slide to your grave.

WOMAN. I can't bear it. I can't bear leaving them. Turn him off. Turn him off.

SCARECROW. (Turning the song off.) Well, maybe you should have thought a bit harder about that before you decided to die.

WOMAN. I didn't decide to die. How dare you?

SCARECROW. You can lie to everyone except me.

WOMAN. It's you who's the liar. I'm sick. The body has caved in, that's all.

SCARECROW. That's all.

WOMAN. My body has betrayed me or I have betrayed it or the betrayal was mutual, who cares, I'm fatal, terminal, hopeless.

SCARECROW. But admit it, you've always loved the idea of dying.

WOMAN. You make it sound like a crime. Yes, in theory death is magnificent but somehow I thought my own would be different.

SCARECROW. It's not up to scratch.

WOMAN. A bit prosaic, all said. It feels more like I'm drifting into a bad-tempered menstrual sleep. Ophelia, now, she had a good death.

SCARECROW. Ophelia died of love.

WOMAN. And what am I dying of?

SCARECROW. Spite.

WOMAN. Spite is an honourable emotion. It's not right up there with love but it's better than dying by accident. Spite has been given bad press for too long. Very well, I'm dying of spite. And since you're such an expert on these matters I'm sure you're going to tell me what it is I am most spiteful about.

SCARECROW. I certainly am. I suppose you could say that your main artery of venom comes from one fact.

WOMAN. Which is?

SCARECROW. That the world has not yielded all you had hoped of it.

WOMAN. Not by a long shot. Yes, that's good. That's as good a reason as any to die. Say it again. I should write that down if I wasn't unconscious.

SCARECROW. The world has not surrendered to you. In fact the world has given you a bit of a battering, I think it's fair to say. But as I keep telling you, it's a question of how you deal with what's thrown in your lap.

WOMAN. I didn't fight back enough. I wasn't brave.

SCARECROW. You copped on too late.

WOMAN. Well, that's something. And what was it I copped onto too late?

SCARECROW. The first law.

WOMAN. What first law?

SCARECROW. You don't know the first law of the world?

WOMAN. Is there one?

SCARECROW. I've told you. I've told you! You never listen.

WOMAN. Tell me again.

SCARECROW. You'll forget again. A waste of time now anyway.

WOMAN. Then tell me because it's a waste of time?

SCARECROW. The first law of the world, which should be nailed on every cot. The first law. The world's job is to take everything from you. Yours is not to let it.

WOMAN. And how have I fared?

SCARECROW. There's no describing what you have given away, wilfully given away. You used up everything you had trying to give everyone what they wanted.

WOMAN. Hence my spite.

SCARECROW. Hence your spite.

WOMAN. I'd prefer to call it bitterness if you've no objections.

SCARECROW. You think bitterness sounds more important?

WOMAN. Bitterness is the aristocracy of spite. Yes, it has a grander ring.

SCARECROW. No matter how you dress it up, it's still nothing to be proud of. You're going into your grave out of bitterness, out of a sense of ruthless meanness, you who were given so much, you who I had such hopes for. I truly believed when I latched on to you before the weaver's throne. I truly believed that you and I would amount to something. I was wrong. Yes, your bitterness was in the weave, but I never thought it would bring us down. It looked such a small inconseqential thing, no more than a slipped stitch.

WOMAN. I've surprised you then.

SCARECROW. You've floored me.

WOMAN. With my boundless capacity for bitterness. Actually boundless is a conservative estimate of my bitterness. Is there a bigger word than boundless?

SCARECROW. Unboundable? Gargantuan rancour? I don't know. I give up.

WOMAN. Do we have a dictionary handy?

SCARECROW. You're too weak to turn the pages. You're almost blind.

WOMAN. Never to read again.

SCARECROW. Correct.

WOMAN. Could we change our minds? Un-die as it were?

SCARECROW. Not since Lazarus has someone un-died.

WOMAN. Am I still breathing?

SCARECROW. Just about.

WOMAN. Do you believe the Lazarus story?

SCARECROW. Oh yes, everything is possible.

WOMAN. Except for me. I'm not important enough to be brought back.

SCARECROW. Neither was Lazarus, sure, who was he, only somebody's little brother. Mary Magdalene's, wasn't it?

WOMAN. Martha and Mary's.

SCARECROW. That's right. The two grannies who hung out with our Lord.

WOMAN. And what did he do after he was brought back?

SCARECROW. What do you mean, what did he do?

WOMAN. Well, how long did he live the second time? Did he drink coffee under the palm trees? Did he terrify the village? Did babies scream and dogs go silent when he walked down the street?

SCARECROW. On that the great book is silent, as it is on all the ordinary unbearable tragedies, because the great miracle of Lazarus is not the pyrotechnics of our Lord. No, the great miracle of Lazarus is that he didn't insist on getting straight back into the coffin.

WOMAN. I take it you don't want to come back.

SCARECROW. That's not what I said.

WOMAN. You dont' want to come back with me? You don't want to go on with me.

SCARECROW. That possibility does not arise.

WOMAN. Well, I wouldn't turn down another sojourn here with or without you.

SCARECROW. I don't believe you.

WOMAN. It's the encroaching annihilation is doing it. I've changed.

SCARECROW. You haven't changed since your holy communion.

WOMAN. You don't know the first thing about me.

SCARECROW. I know when you're lying. Anyway, doesn't matter. Lie away. I'm through with you. I'm just going through the motions. I'll find someone else.

WOMAN. Who will you find?

SCARECROW. Someone with possibility this time. Someone who hasn't surrendered before they're out of nappies.

WOMAN. Did I give up that early?

SCARECROW. I'm exaggerating. I'm a little angry with you. I have loved you for so long. You've never returned it. Threw me a few scraps from time to time. Kept me tagging along on whims and promises, promises that were not kept.

WOMAN. You asked too much. You're still asking it.

SCARECROW. I only asked for a little happiness.

WOMAN. A little happiness!

SCARECROW. You make it sound like some obscure metal.

WOMAN. And is it not?

SCARECROW. No, it's easy to be happy. Happiness like most things is a decision, like going to the dentist or painting a wall. There's no great mystery.

WOMAN. Well, it's a mystery to me and remains one. Maybe my destiny was to be baffled by happiness. You're right. Let's not go on like this. Let's end it all. Bring me the mirror please.

SCARECROW. What do you want the mirror for?

WOMAN. To watch myself die. I want to see how I am. I always look in mirrors to find out what's happening to me. Please bring me the mirror. I want to see if I'm still here.

SCARECROW. You want to drool over the vestiges of your beauty.

WOMAN. Then let me drool. Thank God I still have my vanity.

SCARECROW. *(Bringing her the mirror.)* Not much left to feed your vanity now. Look at you, your bones are pushing through your skin.

WOMAN. Are they? Show? I can't see. At last. That's wonderful. There's not much about this century I'd go on bended knee to, but to its ideal of beauty I will. Both of them. Bones, teeth, hair, the age adores. Well, I always had good teeth and despite everything my hair is still magnificent. And now finally I have achieved bones. My dear I have transformed myself into the ideal. Look at me, I am graveyard chic, angular, lupine, dangerous. *(Raises an arm, turns it, lifts a leg, admires it.)* Look at these arms, these legs, the contours of these limbs. I am slowly carving myself into a Greek statue. All those slices of bread and jam, all those pots of spuds and butter, all that apple tart and cream, all fallen away. Admire me for once in my skeletal queenality.

SCARECROW. You're determined to provoke me.

WOMAN. And yet some of my greatest memories are of food. Roast beef with gravy and mash. Mackerel straight from the sea, so fresh you could taste the waves trapped within the meat. What else? Salmon sashimi with pickled ginger … foie gras … what was it served with again?

12

SCARECROW. Melon, I think, on a bed of lettuce.

WOMAN. And I refused to share it. Devoured it. Who was it bought me the foie gras?

SCARECROW. The one that wanted you to parade naked around the room.

WOMAN. And did I?

SCARECROW. You did.

WOMAN. Pity I don't remember it then. Was I happy? Parading naked around the room?

SCARECROW. Too much of the convent psychic in you to enjoy parading naked anywhere.

WOMAN. It's wonderful to have such a critical spectator on all one's most intimate journeys. Was he the same one used to watch this video of a shark before he made love?

SCARECROW. That was the German in the cowboy boots.

WOMAN. That's right. The German. He was a magnificent specimen of a man, wasn't he?

SCARECROW. Yes, he had big bones.

WOMAN. Six-foot-four in his stocking feet. And he kept rewinding to this shot of the shark erupting out of the water, the big maw of him and his hundreds of razor teeth. And then he'd freeze-frame the close-up of the shark's mouth and just lie there looking at it. Good God, I know what he was doing. He was fantasising that I was the shark.

SCARECROW. That only dawning on you now?

WOMAN. And he had mirrors all over the room and when we'd part he'd always say, "*Ciao bella.*" Strange, that, for a German. "*Ciao bella,*" just like that and he'd drive off, never saying when we'd meet again. And when I wouldn't anymore, couldn't anymore, I think I was pregnant again, yes, that must have been it. He kept calling for ages.

SCARECROW. An act of revenge, that's all he was, that's what they all were, just acts of revenge. Your heart wasn't involved. I wasn't allowed a look in.

WOMAN. They were more than that. In the beginning maybe, but they were more than that. They were more than revenge.

SCARECROW. And I'm telling you they weren't. Your backward, twisted little heart was tied, always tied to him who made little of you every opportunity he could.

WOMAN. He wasn't always like that.

SCARECROW. Remember what Auntie Ah said.

WOMAN. Yes, I remember.

SCARECROW. Tell me what she said.

WOMAN. If you know, why're you asking me?

SCARECROW. Just tell me.

WOMAN. No.

SCARECROW. Then I'll tell you. I'd rather see your white body floating down the Shannon than for you to marry that man.

WOMAN. Well, I'm glad you've got that off your chest.

SCARECROW. And twenty-five years later, would you agree with Auntie Ah's pronouncement?

WOMAN. Oh yes.

SCARECROW. You admit she was right?

WOMAN. I've always known it. From the start I knew this man is no good for me.

SCARECROW. And you went ahead?

WOMAN. Yes I did.

SCARECROW. Why?

WOMAN. Because my dress was made and everyone was invited.

SCARECROW. Because your dress was made you had eight children.

WOMAN. I'd have had twenty if he wanted.

SCARECROW. But he didn't want.

WOMAN. That's not true. He's fond of them in a distracted sort of way.

SCARECROW. I can't make head nor tail of you.

WOMAN. It's all confusion, Scarecrow.

SCARECROW. Can I just ask you one thing?

WOMAN. One can always ask.

SCARECROW. After all he's done …

WOMAN. Don't start in on him again.

SCARECROW. Let me finish.

WOMAN. Alright.

SCARECROW. Do you love him still?

WOMAN. Of course not.

SCARECROW. I don't believe you.

WOMAN. If I say, "Yes, I still love him" you'll throttle me.

SCARECROW. I won't.

WOMAN. I know you.

SCARECROW. I promise I won't go near you. I just want to know the lie of the land. Do you love him still?

WOMAN. I don't know … yes … I adore him.

SCARECROW. Good God. *(Hands over her face.)*
WOMAN. It's terrible, is it?
SCARECROW. You've no idea.
WOMAN. Then tell me.
SCARECROW. No, I want you to go peacefully, without fear.
WOMAN. And how am I doing on the peaceful scale? On the fear gauge? *(Scarecrow just looks at her.)* You see terrors ahead. Well, I'll meet them when I meet them. At least the terrors of the Earth are over. It can't be worse than here … can it? *(Scarecrow doesn't answer.)* Well, you can just take that smug eternal look off your face or look away. Look away. Don't look at me like that, as if you know something. If you know something, tell me.
SCARECROW. You don't want to know.
WOMAN. You can't wait to fly off, dump me in the grave, fly off with him.
SCARECROW. I assure you, I have no desire to fly off with that thing in the wardrobe. I promised you I'd settle you into your grave. I have never yet broken a promise to you. Can you say the same?
WOMAN. Then why am I afraid to close my eyes?
SCARECROW. Close them, I'll watch.
WOMAN. You'll sneak away.
SCARECROW. Trust me.
WOMAN. I need to sleep. Promise.
SCARECROW. I told you.
WOMAN. Lie beside me. Hold my hand.
SCARECROW. Don't be such a coward.
WOMAN. And if I don't wake.
SCARECROW. You'll wake.
WOMAN. Swear it.
SCARECROW. I swear.
WOMAN. Okay so … *(Mumbles as she drifts off.)* And the mountains … what can I say about the mountains except they were there and they were beautiful … purple on brown on blue on Parma grey, isn't that what they call it … and the memory of ice in the light on the water and the water glass … was that out west, or did I just dream it and the dwarf oaks shaped by storm, bent and rounded as old women's backs, hopeless, hopeless … or is there such a thing as light at all … And the whole landscape, the mountain, the tree, the water, poised, waiting for something … ah yes, now I know what the mountain was waiting for, waiting for us to

depart and leave it alone again with the sky … they don't need us; they never have and they never will. *(And she drifts off. Scarecrow watches her a minute, goes to wardrobe, puts her ear to the door, listens. Enter Him. He goes to bed, kisses Woman, who sleeps.)*

HIM. Wake up … come on … *(Rouses her gently.)*

WOMAN. *(Takes his hand.)* How long have I been here?

HIM. Since Thursday … we found you on Thursday. Why did you run off like that?

WOMAN. I wanted to go back to where I came from.

HIM. You don't want to be here with me, with the children.

WOMAN. I was here for decades — too late now, I don't see too well anymore. I wouldn't see the sea.

HIM. Can you see me?

WOMAN. Yes, I can see you.

HIM. Are you in pain, my dear? *(Woman looks at Scarecrow. They burst out laughing.)* What is it? Let me in on the joke. *(They continue laughing.)* You're high as a kite. Maybe I should take a slug of this, too. *(He pours medicine into a beaker, lifts Woman's head. She drinks. He lays her back on the pillow.)*

WOMAN. Thank you. *(Scarecrow turns her eyes up to heaven.)*

HIM. *(Smoothes Woman's hair.)* My dear, I haven't treated you as I should have and now there isn't time.

SCARECROW. You have had abundance of time.

HIM. Can you forgive my callous treatment of you?

WOMAN. *(To Scarecrow.)* Can I?

SCARECROW. Since when have you considered my opinion?

WOMAN. Your callous treatment of me. Did you rehearse that phrase?

HIM. Did I what?

WOMAN. It was more than callous. Don't pretty it up for a deathbed.

HIM. Can you forgive me, my dear?

WOMAN. What does it matter whether I forgive or don't forgive?

HIM. Oh, it matters. And will matter more when you're gone.

SCARECROW. He makes your death sound like an infidelity.

WOMAN. And is it not?

SCARECROW. Then no, if it matters, no forgiveness. Let him suffer a little. Ask him why he kept returning.

WOMAN. Why did you keep returning?

HIM. Because you are my wife, because you are the mother of my children, because despite how it appears, you have always and will always be the one.

WOMAN. If you only lived how your speak. I don't believe it anymore. You kept coming back because you know I would never have the courage to leave you, to bar the door, to break my children's hearts. You are suffocating me.

HIM. You know I will remember what you're saying now when you're gone.

WOMAN. Yes, remember it.

HIM. You hve a duty to leave me softly as I have a duty to watch you go without rancor.

WOMAN. I am drowning in duty.

HIM. And what am I?

WOMAN. Just play something for me. I don't want to talk to you now.

HIM. My dear, talk to me … forgive me … I will have to carry you with me until the end.

WOMAN. Play something.

HIM. All right … what would you like to hear?

WOMAN. Something romantic. There has been too little romance in my life.

HIM. I'll leave the door open. *(He exits. In a minute we hear piano music. They listen a while.)*

SCARECROW. You played it better when you played.

WOMAN. I never cared. Yes, I played it better when I played.

SCARECROW. And then you stopped.

WOMAN. And then I stopped.

SCARECROW. He didn't like you playing.

WOMAN. I played when he wasn't here. A bottle of champagne open, the children asleep, just you and me. No, I suppose he never like me to do anything better than him.

SCARECROW. Deal with that at the door of the tomb.

WOMAN. How should I deal with it?

SCARECROW. You martyred yourself to a mediocrity.

WOMAN. Ssh, listen … He does remorse very well. You have to give him that. Give him that at least.

SCARECROW. He's the high priest of remorse. He's jealous of your death. He's determined to wring the most he can from it. If you're not careful, he'll hijack your last breath.

WOMAN. No, he's more fragile than that. I've carried him and his shattered ego for years. He's more exhausting than all the children put together … Tell me, you who have an nswer for everything, tell me what it is about dying that's so sexy?

SCARECROW. You think this is sexy?

WOMAN. Is there a moon in the sky? The music, my extinction, what is it?

SCARECROW. A chance to be epic, I suppose. Life withholds the epic. Until the end.

WOMAN. Then let's enjoy it. We only get to do it once.

SCARECROW. I'm not in an epic mood.

WOMAN. Why not?

SCARECROW. Too many things about you are small.

WOMAN. Epicness is for the brave, the beautiful.

SCARECROW. You had it once. When you were a fat teenager with permed hair. You knew then what epic was and epic asked.

WOMAN. And then what happened to me?

SCARECROW. You turned chicken and fled the battlefield.

WOMAN. I fought the good fight if you didn't. I have the scars to prove it.

SCARECROW. Skirmishes. Merely skirmishes.

WOMAN. Whatever. Open the wine. This orgy of sobriety is killing me. Open the wine.

SCARECROW. Your throat is almost closed. You'll choke.

WOMAN. Wine's as good as anything to choke on.

SCARECROW. Okay, let's open the wine. *(Takes a bottle of wine from locker. Opens it.)* The wine from him.

WOMAN. Which him?

SCARECROW. Which him? The him that should have been THE HIM.

WOMAN. Oh, him. His parting gift. Okay, let's drink it then. The wine and the diamond ring. The big rock. Where is it?

SCARECROW. I'm wearing it.

WOMAN. And the song and dance under the weeping willows, I couldn't wait to get away … a little wiry fella … of no consequence really.

SCARECROW. He borrowed a fortune to buy you this ring.

WOMAN. Yes, I had it valued … was going to sell it … I don't know why I didn't.

SCARECROW. He loved you. More. He loved me. He saw past your tattered hide. He saw you as you should be seen. He saw

me and he loved me. But you couldn't handle that, jealous sur-
face bitch that you are. You'd sooner listen to that barbarian
murder Chopin than live and let me live too. *(Brandishes diamond ring.)*

WOMAN. I didn't know you were so taken with him.

SCARECROW. He would have kept us alive.

WOMAN. I suppose I did use him a bit when things were desper-
ate here, but my car broke down. I was never meant to even meet
him … just one of those things … he was very kind but kindess
can be a nuisance after a while … anyway, the children.

SCARECROW. The excuse for everything. Here. *(Hands her a
glass of wine. Woman can barely hold it.)* Drink his wine and think
you could be with him now. I could be with him now instead of
this funeral parlour.

WOMAN. Can you hold it for me … feed it to me. *(Scarecrow
does, Woman takes a sip.)* Cheers.

SCARECROW. Cheer me, no cheers.

WOMAN. Beautiful wine. The planets' last connection to the gods.

SCARECROW. Might I ask what we're celebrating?

WOMAN. It'll come to us eventually.

SCARECROW. Will we chance a fag?

WOMAN. Cigarettes are your fault.

SCARECROW. Cigarettes were the only time I ever got you on
your own. Yes, let's chance a fag. Where are they?

WOMAN. There was a packet in my dressing gown, oh, a hundred years ago.

SCARECROW. I'll smoke for both of us.

WOMAN. No, if there are cigarettes on the table I want in on them.

SCARECROW. In a minute.

WOMAN. Now!

SCARECROW. Ask me nicely.

WOMAN. I'm sick of you. I'm so sick of you.

SCARECROW. Your mood has changed. You have wine. You have
cigarettes, or the memory of them. Just imagine, you could be sitting with him. Alive. By a big fire, your children roaming the
house. You were meant for a long life. Okay, have a puff.

WOMAN. Get away. I don't want one now.

SCARECROW. I thought we were having a party. Your mood has
changed.

WOMAN. That's what moods are for. For changing. You'd have

me on an even keel twelve months of the year. Yes, my mood has changed. Sometimes wine does that. Sobers you.

SCARECROW. Come on, drink up. *(Holds glass for Woman. Woman takes a sip.)*

WOMAN. Who was it recommended three glasses of wine a day?

SCARECROW. That was Keats. Three glasses. No more. No less.

WOMAN. I wonder what size the glasses were in the romantic era.

SCARECROW. The romantic era wasn't very romantic for Keats.

WOMAN. At least he left something after him.

SCARECROW. Aren't you leaving a brood of them? Maybe they'll amount to something.

WOMAN. When did it all turn to tragedy? When did I stop lampooning the world? And why?

WOMAN. This wine is no good. Death should be intoxicating.

SCARECROW. Have another sip. It may lift the fog. We mustn't meet the darkness with the dark.

WOMAN. I look over the years and all I see is one wrong turn leading to another wrong turn. I cannot remember a moment when it was right.

SCARECROW. Your mind is a swill.

WOMAN. A sewer. Let it not erupt. Can I just go now?

SCARECROW. Slip away mid-sentence is it?

WOMAN. Before we're interrupted again. They're all out there lining up for a gawk. I heard an argument over brass handles, must be for my coffin. Can I just go?

SCARECROW. If that's what you really want.

WOMAN. I'll stop breathing so. *(Puts covers over her head.)* It'll be easier this way. Right. On the count of three.

SCARECROW. No final soliloquies.

WOMAN. *(Head out from under covers.)* What?

SCARECROW. No farewell speech.

WOMAN. None. *(Back under covers.)* Okay. One. Two. Three. Good-bye, Scarecrow.

SCARECROW. Yeah. *(Hold a minute. Scarecrow begins to suffer, doesn't fall this time. Enter Auntie Ah.)*

AUNTIE AH. So it's come to this.

WOMAN. So it has.

AUNTIE AH. I put your mother in the ground, too.

WOMAN. Where is she buried?

AUNTIE AH. You don't know where your own mother is buried?

WOMAN. No, where exactly in the graveyard? I could never her grave when I went looking after.

AUNTIE AH. It was in the south corner but graveyards changing.

WOMAN. There were the elms. And the sun slanting through. Came away empty-handed. Never had the wherewithal to face it again. I left the children fighting in the car. Was afraid to take them to her grave. I thought somehow she would suck them in. I needn't have worried. Not a trace of her. Did you even put up a tombstone?

AUNTIE AH. Why didn't you go to a doctor sooner? There's no call for this nonsense. I could've laid down too more times than I care to recount, but it wasn't for nothing I grew up on the western seaboard, a grey land of rock and thistle where little or nothing thrives. And it wasn't for nothing you were born there too. But the eastern blood of your father diluted the limestone and softened you to this. Would you not sit up and have a bowl of stew and put an end to this nonsense? And what's in store for your chickens now? You think to fling them on the walls of the world and have the rest of us pick up the broken bones. Your mother was the same. No finishing power. Anyone can get through the first half. You start a life. You finish it. You don't bail out at the crossroads because you don't like the scenery. It's weak. I despise it. And I'll tell you something else, my niece of a girl, there'll be no ecstasies at the finish. I've handed many of them back to their Maker and not a one of them sang as the curtain fell. They went confused, they went jabbering, they went silent, they went howling, but not one of them went with the beatified light in the eye as if they'd seen a vision of something pleasing. All I ever saw was the light draining from the basalt of the eyeball, the light draining. And the light gone. I'm leaving five thousand under the pillow, sure you can't even afford to die.

WOMAN. It's not many would offer you the price of your own funeral and you still breathing.

AUNTIE AH. Delicate sentiments. Delicate sentiments. And what do they weigh against a bag of gold? You've them all destroyed back west with this piece of foolishness. I will not forgive this. I will not. This willful jaunt to your doom. (*And exit Auntie Ah trailing her knitting.*)

SCARECROW. Were those tears? Auntie Ah in tears. Could she

21

possibly miss us?

WOMAN. She only loves hanging out of the dying, laid out half of Connemarra. She's looking forward to the whole catastrophe.

SCARECROW. Alas, poor Yorick.

WOMAN. Alas indeed. Only if we're lucky will it end in the grave.

SCARECROW. You're afraid of that, aren't you?

WOMAN. Waking in the coffin with the serpent at my breast ... Yes, I'm afraid of that.

SCARECROW. Or the rats boring through the plywood, their paws on your face.

WOMAN. My belly a pudding of worms.

SCARECROW. And you awake the whole time. Watching the serpent and the rat and the worms have their smelly feast.

WOMAN. They will start with the softest parts ... the eyes.

SCARECROW. Then with their claws will scoop out the meat of your brain.

WOMAN. Then the ears.

SCARECROW. The lips.

WOMAN. The tongue.

SCARECROW. They will part your stomach like wet paper and reach for the heart, the breasts, the intestine.

WOMAN. The kidneys, the womb, the ovaries, they will wrap themselves around my lungs and suck out the tripe of my spine.

SCARECROW. And so on.

WOMAN. How long will this last?

SCARECROW. *Hamlet*'s gravedigger says ... is it eight years? Seems overlong to me.

WOMAN. Let's trust the bard. Eight years 'til we're clean as Yorick. And then?

SCARECROW. Perhaps the real torture will begin.

WOMAN. That has always been a possibility. All my life I've been afraid of rats. At last I know why.

SCARECROW. Some poet or other said rats backwards is star.

WOMAN. And poet backwards is stop.

SCARECROW. Stop backwards is pots.

WOMAN. Pots is even better.

WOMAN. There is nothing star-like about rats. Filthy creatures and no wonder when we are their staple diet. I think I'll ask him to cremate me. Better the conflagration of hair and nails and crackling gristle than a banquet for rats. I read somewhere they have an intricate tunnel system from grave to grave. No, the roar of the furnace and then it's over. Scatter me on the wind, and who's to say I won't become a particle of some new galaxy trying to be born. *(Enter Him.)*

HIM. Is there anything I can do? Turn you? Will I turn you?

WOMAN. *(Nods and then to Scarecrow.)* Don't look at me, you.

SCARECROW. I can look.

HIM. *(Turning her.)* Let me raise the pillows too. So quiet, my dear, and so calm. What are you thinking?

WOMAN. Always the same, about my happiness and my unhappiness.

HIM. Are you?

WOMAN. No. That's what Anna Karenina said. I've always wanted to say it … I was thinking of the house I grew up in.

SCARECROW. You were not.

HIM. You grew up in many houses.

WOMAN. The first one. My mother's and father's house. From upstairs you could see right across the bay. Why did we never make it back to the sea?

HIM. I've missed the sea too.

WOMAN. Maybe we would've been better people there.

HIM. Maybe we would.

WOMAN. At the very least the sea would've added some sort of grandeur to all of this. The day my mother died … her infant son dead beside her … they were going to call him Michael … I never saw him … and I always meant to find out which of them died first.

SCARECROW. What does it matter which of them went first? They went. They went. What more is there to know?

WOMAN. There is much, much more to know.

HIM. What, my dear? What is it you want to know?

WOMAN. Grief can be measured. Grief can be calibrated. But I'm not talking to you, stop butting in. I want to tell him something.

SCARECROW. You think this man is interested in the heart-breaking details of your life.

WOMAN. You give him credit for nothing.

HIM. What is it? You're all agitated. What is it you want to tell me?

WOMAN. I forget … she drives me mad … oh yes … that day.

The day she died. Daddy and I went in on the bus. A scorcher of a day, but still I insisted on wearing my red coat and red hat. I wanted to wear it because a couple of days before my mother and I had spent a whole day trying on coats for me. We went from shop to shop, but no coat satisfied her. She had in her mind this red coat and red hat that failed to materialise. We went to Lydons for tea and cream buns. Her mood was sombre, belligerent even. It was getting late. The shops would be closed soon. She stared out the window and mumbled something about it being a bloody miracle if we found it now. Her voice so low, defeated, the huge hump of her belly wedged against the table, her shoes kicked off because they pained her. I can't remember where we found the coat. Her hands shook as she did up the black velvet buttons. She led me to a mirror. "Now look at yourself," she said, "just look at yourself." But it is her I see now, her girth disappearing in dusty shadow, old before her time and still radiant, the white teeth flashing, the russet gold of her hair and the expression in her eyes. I in my new red coat and hat gave her pleasure. Pleasure beyond describing. For one brief moment, a mirror glance, I was that thing she had yearned for and found. *(Bursts into tears.)*

HIM. My dear. My dear.

WOMAN. Do me the honour of not comforting me where there can be no comfort. *(He watches helplessly as Woman weeps and weeps, a protracted grieving of sound and liquid. This eventually subsides. He pours some medicine into a beaker.)* Get away from me with that. It makes me crazy.

HIM. But the pains will return.

WOMAN. It numbs me. I can't feel anything anymore.

HIM. I can't have you suffering.

WOMAN. For twenty-five years you've caused my suffering. For once in your life speak the truth.

HIM. And what truth is that?

WOMAN. You've wanted me dead for years.

HIM. This is crazy talk.

WOMAN. But it's true.

HIM. No, it's not true.

WOMAN. Then tell me one true thing. I don't care how brutal it is.

HIM. Just stop this. You're upsetting yourself for no reason.

WOMAN. You've just been with her.

HIM. Alright, you want the unvarnished truth. I've just been with her. She's parked up the road. Now leave it please. Leave it at that. It's no good thing going over and over it.

WOMAN. And afteryou pour that stuff into me, knock me out, you'll go back out to her.

HIM. Yes, I'll go back out to her. She's taking me for a quick dinner before I go mad here.

WOMAN. Go then. Go! There are others who can provide less venomous care.

HIM. Your relations! The house is falling down with them. A big coven of witches in *báinín* and black. They've eaten everything, drunk everything. I've had to borrow money from my mother. Right now they're devouring the stew I made for the children. Last night they got through eight bottles of whiskey. They hang out in the bathroom smoking and shrieking. The children aren't talking to me because I won't let them go clubbing. They haven't been to school in weeks. We're all waiting. We're all waiting. Die if you're going to. If not, get up.

WOMAN. I don't want her at my funeral.

HIM. Don't worry. I'm finishing with her too. If she thinks I'm going to set up house with her when you're gone. I said it right out to her. What's the point in changing horses? Is that honest enough for you or will I go on? *(Woman just stares at him.)* You drive me to the limit every time so I say things that shouldn't be said … Look, take this stuff … it's revenge enough you're going. Must I watch you go howling?

WOMAN. If that's what it takes.

HIM. There are many ways to leave someone. Mine is a cliché. I lack your savagery. You chose to leave me while staying to view the wreckage.

WOMAN. I want you to know I've had my flings too.

HIM. You have not.

WOMAN. You think I was just sitting here pining for you.

HIM. You're raving. You want to destroy me.

WOMAN. It astonishes you anyone would want me.

HIM. I didn't say that.

WOMAN. But you're thinking it. Believe it or not, you wanted me yourself once.

HIM. Right now that is hard to believe.

WOMAN. Several sorties in fact.

HIM. You're just trying to make me jealous.

WOMAN. I'm not trying to make you anything.

HIM. How dare you?

WOMAN. How dare I what?

HIM. Lying like this. You want to leave me with nothing. I have to live. I have to look after those children. How dare you sully us like this?

WOMAN. You don't believe me.

HIM. It can't be true.

WOMAN. Do you want names? Telephone numbers?

HIM. You are capable of that?

WOMAN. Yes, I am capable of that … of afternoons in other men's house … showering and perfuming for a stranger's arms … You think I survived this long on the scraps you threw me?

HIM. All the time acting the weeping virgin, the woman abandoned. How dare you.

WOMAN. Oh I dared, and I'll tell you something else, if it wasn't for the children I'd have walked years ago. Take these. *(Throws rings at him.)* Sell them. Buy some more food and drink for my crowd. At least they know how to celebrate, ignorant old crones that they are. But they know this much. A person's passing is a sacred thing and merits some kind of overdose. So serve them well and let them drink and feast and sing me to my final place. Go! Look after them. You might learn something.

HIM. I have dirges a-plenty too, if you'd only listen.

WOMAN. I've listened to you too long and all that listening has taught me nothing.

HIM. Nothing?

WOMAN. Nothing. Save. You were not worthy of my love.

HIM. So that's the way of it?

WOMAN. You drank the wine. Now drink the vinegar.

HIM. Just one thing you have never understood. You mistook, deliberately mistook my roving for rejection.

WOMAN. Roving! It was annihilation. Annihilation of me. Roving!

HIM. I never withdrew from you. Never. You were the one slammed like a thousand doors as only a woman can. *(And exit Him in a storm.)*

SCARECROW. He's almost tolerable when he stands up for himself.

WOMAN. I'm out of control. I won't be happy until I've ground him into the dirt.

SCARECROW. Validation of oneself sometimes involves that.

26

WOMAN. Right now nothing will satisy but to bring him down with me. Oh, Scarecrow, I'm so afraid.

SCARECROW. Afraid is Disneyland.

WOMAN. Terrified?

SCARECROW. Horrified and every other ide.

WOMAN. I am murderous with my own passing.

SCARECROW. Close. You're getting close.

WOMAN. I see tombs in shadow, mossy, weather-scarred tombs and all the dead squashed in and me with them wondering if there is starlight above.

SCARECROW. Shush for a while 'til we try and articulate it right. *(A pause. The wardrobe door creaks open. Woman and Scarecrow turn to look, a wing appears from the wardrobe, then a clawed foot, then lights down.)*

End of Act One

ACT TWO

Woman lies in bed with blood trickling down her chin. She clasps a bunch of black feathers in her hand. Sounds of battle from the wardrobe.

WOMAN. *(Weakly.)* Scarecrow! … Scarecrow … are you alright? *(Battle increases in frenzy from wardrobe: grunts, cries of pain, growls, pants, howls.)* What is that thing doing to you? *(Enter Auntie Ah.)*

AUNTIE AH. There's blood on your mouth.

WOMAN. He came at me with his beak. I pulled at his feathers. *(Woman holds up a clump of black feathers.)*

AUNTIE AH. Where did you get those?

WOMAN. I just told you.

AUNTIE AH. Let me swab your mouth. *(Cleans Woman up, straightens bed, sheets, pillows.)*

WOMAN. It's going to kill her.

AUNTIE AH. The state of the room, swear there was a wrestling match here.

WOMAN. Get her! Get her! Help her! Scarecrow's still in the wardrobe.

AUNTIE AH. Ah, there's always someone in the wardrobe. Come on, we'll say a decade of the rosary.

WOMAN. *(Calls.)* Scarecrow, would a rosary help?

AUNTIE AH. *(Taking out beads.)* Oh Lord, open my lips so my tongue can announce Thy praise.

WOMAN. I said desist in your crazy orisions.

AUNTIE AH. You're above the old prayers, is that it? Above God? Above the Blue Virgin and her entourage of bird men. What'll you say when you alight above and this sacrilege is played before you like a newsreel?

WOMAN. And what of His sacrilege against me?

AUNTIE AH. What sacrilege?

WOMAN. Well, how about you for starters?

AUNTIE AH. No need to take your bad temper out on God or

on me.

WOMAN. God is for the living.

AUNTIE AH. God is for all time.

WOMAN. In the Louvre there is a painting, the Italian section. I saw it last summer. Imagine, last summer I was strolling Paris. I drank glass after glass of Sancerre. I flirted. I smoked. I ate raw steak 'til the blood dribbled down my chin and I looked beautiful, Paris is the correct backdrop for me. I was set free, a woman with eight children roaming Paris. Why did I bother coming back? Scarecrow, are you still alive? … What are you doing?

AUNTIE AH. Stop blathering, you're dying, not going mad. Focus your mind, girl, you were telling me about smoking and flirting in Paris.

WOMAN. Many lifetimes ago and I went every day across the Seine to see the Caravaggio. *The Death of the Virgin.* Her feet were blue. Her dress was red. Everyone has their head bowed. Oh their grief, terrible to look on, frightening. And you know why, Auntie Ah? Because the miracle is over. She's going down into the clay, not up to the blue beyond. The Apostles know it. Caravaggio knows it and we know it.

AUNTIE AH. Her feet were blue. What sort of a painter is that? You mean her dress was blue.

WOMAN. Yes, blue is too kind. Her feet were more a putrid greeny black. Bad circulation maybe, varicose veins or maybe he was just faithfully recording the rot. She looks about fifty. And still there is something sacred going on. Not with her. She's just another of those invisible women past their prime. But the mourners are appalling … put the heart crossways in you, Auntie Ah.

AUNTIE AH. Would it, girl?

WOMAN. She was the last mortal loved by a god. And with her end came the end of God's desire for any truck with us. The funeral bier of the last mortal some god briefly and casually loved. But do you know what amazes me, Auntie Ah?

AUNTIE AH. What?

WOMAN. That He was here so recently.

AUNTIE AH. And won't you be lying in His arms before this night descends?

WOMAN. That is too much to hope for from here. Something I've always been meaning to ask you, Auntie Ah.

AUNTIE AH. Ask away, girl.

WOMAN. Why do they always have graveyards on the beaches in Connemarra?

AUNTIE AH. For fear we'd enjoy the sun or sand too much.

WOMAN. We should all live beside graveyards, otherwise we're likely to forget.

AUNTIE AH. Forget what?

WOMAN. That the whole point of living is preparing to die. Why did no one ever teach me that?

AUNTIE AH. I did.

WOMAN. You did not. You were all simper and gush about heaven. Had to figure it out for myself. Too late of course. And now to be cut off in the blossom of my sins.

AUNTIE AH. Now you're talking. Father Gant is in the kitchen waiting on your confession.

WOMAN. He'll be waiting.

AUNTIE AH. It's the height of bad manners. Confess for my sake. Sure what could you be guilty of except ignorance and greed and cruelty to your relations and a bit of robbery from time to time. You used to rob from my handbag. Did you ever confess that? You think I didn't notice. I noticed and thought to store it up for the future. Confess now and confess all and you'll be able to look your Maker in the eye instead of hanging back slyly in the crowd, hoping He'll have forgotten your transgressions. He won't, you know. Good girl, confess.

WOMAN. It's a terrible state of affairs to arrive at the close of your life and realise you've nothing to confess. Though looked at the proper way, I suppose I committed the greatest sin of all.

AUNTIE AH. What sin are you talking about?

WOMAN. I wasn't good to myself … I wasn't happy.

AUNTIE AH. I remember you happy. Your holy communion, the day you left on the train to go up to university. Wild horses wouldn't stop you.

WOMAN. That wasn't happiness. That was relief getting away from you.

AUNTIE AH. It was happiness. I have the snapshots to prove it and countless memories of you laughing yourself silly as a girl. But that's what's wrong today, everyone thinks they have a God-given right to happiness. It's only a recent invention of the Sunday newspapers. It'll wither and pass in time and we'll go back to the way we were.

WOMAN. Scarecrow ... Scarecrow ... come back ... I need you. What are you still hovering for?

AUNTIE AH. I have earned the right to hover. It is not my fault you never allowed me to be your mother.

WOMAN. You want to ogle me off the planet.

AUNTIE AH. I'll admit I'm curious. I like to see the finish of a life. How we die says it all about how we have lived. I'll lay you out. I won't let strangers near you. And I'll do what I can for your children.

WOMAN. Oh, Auntie Ah, don't make me savage you. I don't have the energy. Please just keep away from my children.

AUNTIE AH. The times have softened me with them. The terrible rages are gone, woke one morning and all the anger, just flown.

WOMAN. What's flown, what's fleeting are those you inflicted them upon. *(Door of wardrobe opens. Scarecrow steps out, covered in blood and bruises, nightdress torn.)*

SCARECROW. *(Softly to the wardrobe.)* Yes. Yes. Thank you. *(A low growling sound from wardrobe.)* I never thought you were.

WOMAN. What did it do to you?

SCARECROW. Don't you ever accuse me again of not loving you ... I bartered myself for more time.

WOMAN. How much time?

SCARECROW. Half an hour.

WOMAN. Half an hour!

SCARECROW. You should've seen what it wanted for an hour. I couldn't do it.

WOMAN. Should I go in? What can anyone do with half an hour?

SCARECROW. Or a century for that matter. What can be done with a paltry hundred years?

WOMAN. He can stuff his half hour. I refuse to enjoy it.

SCARECROW. Who's talking about enjoyment?

WOMAN. You told me that's what time was for.

SCARECROW. That was when we had time.

WOMAN. And now we don't?

SCARECROW. That's correct.

WOMAN. After half an hour there's no more half hours.

SCARECROW. What in the name of God did I ever see in you?

WOMAN. One could make love in half an hour.

SCARECROW. One could if one had a lover.

WOMAN. Why didn't I have more sex when I could have?

SCARECROW. You were too busy hoovering.

WOMAN. These battered old hands have not touched enough.

SCARECROW. No, none of that will happen again.

WOMAN. You needn't sound so final about it. And my dreams were all of infidelity. Strange, that, and I thought I loved him, but my dreams were all of escape, flying, bedding strangers. Why was that, Miss Know-all?

SCARECROW. I was trying to prod you on, to hoick you from this half existence.

WOMAN. What else must I acknowledge?

SCARECROW. That you're a liar.

WOMAN. What do we have? Minutes? Seconds? Auntie Ah, I think I'm pregnant. Three months. It'll go to the grave with me.

AUNTIE AH. Aren't you too old to be pregnant?

WOMAN. It's either that or the menopause.

SCARECROW. Ask her, did you ever have a red coat?

WOMAN. You know well I had.

SCARECROW. Ask her.

WOMAN. Alright, just to prove you wrong. I know what you're insinuating. You look like some Siberian convict out of Dostoevsky. Auntie Ah, did I ever have a red coat?

AUNTIE AH. (Smoothes Woman's hair.) Calm. Calm. Calm, girl. You'll need the vestiages of your mind to orient beyond.

SCARECROW. A red coat and a red hat to match? When I came to you?

AUNTIE AH. You came with only the clothes on your back.

SCARECROW. I knew you made it up. That baloney about the red coat. It never happened.

WOMAN. Now you're going to hijack my memories. Don't you start!

SCARECROW. Why would you lie like that?

WOMAN. Are you telling me there was no moment with my mother on the day she died?

SCARECROW. There was a moment alright, but that wasn't it.

WOMAN. That was a defining moment and now you want to take it from me.

SCARECROW. Why not tell it as it was? You did visit the hospital that day.

WOMAN. It wasn't a hospital. It was a private nursing home.

AUNTIE AH. Above the midwife, she was. I laid her out too.

WOMAN. And I was wearing my new red coat and my new red hat.

SCARECROW. *(Shakes her.)* You were not!

WOMAN. Okay. Okay. Let me think. I wasn't wearing my new red coat and new red hat. I'd left them in the wardrobe on account of the heat.

SCARECROW. No wardrobe. No coat. No hat.

WOMAN. Then what was I wearing?

SCARECROW. It's not important.

WOMAN. Details are all I have. The larger canvas has eluded me. Leave me the details.

SCARECROW. I'll leave you details that are true.

WOMAN. Then tell me what I'm wearing. What did I look like? I can't see myself.

SCARECROW. Can you see her? *(A pause ... a long pause.)*

WOMAN. Yes ... I can see her.

SCARECROW. And what is she doing?

WOMAN. She's sleeping.

SCARECROW. What else?

WOMAN. Nothing else. She's sleeping. Her mouth is open. Her tongue is moving as if she's sucking on something.

SCARECROW. And then?

WOMAN. I go to her.

SCARECROW. *(Whispers.)* No. No. No.

WOMAN. I stand at the door. I just stand there looking at her. I've never seen her asleep before. She's on her side. The sheets are hard and white. Her mouth is open, her tongue is moving. Her hair is flat across the pillow as if someone had ironed it and nailed it there. And that's all ... surely that can't be all?

SCARECROW. There's more.

WOMAN. The basin. The daffodils.

SCARECROW. Yes, but something else.

WOMAN. Yes ... something else ... As I stand there, a terrible realisation comes flashing through ... a picture from the future ... as I stand there, I see myself here, now. I see my own death day ... and now she wakes and looks at me. I swim in her eye, she in mine, we're spellbound, unsmiling, conspirators too wise to fight what has been decreed on high long long ago.

AUNTIE AH. The old people at home used to say when a person was mortally fading, if they could hold on 'til the tide turns they'll surely make it, because there's a moment of grace when the ocean pauses, and in that moment of grace anything can happen.

WOMAN. And did my mother go as the tide turned?

AUNTIE AH. I don't know but the day she died I saw her walking across the sand. I can't explain it. I can't prove it and I still don't believe it, but she was suddenly there, walking up to me and we had words. Or rather I spoke to her, something like, I thought you were beyond in Galway. But she touched my head and whatever way she laid out her hand and touched my head silenced me and then she continued walking. A farewell I suppose, if you believe in that sort of thing. Yes, that's what it was. She married your father on the rebound but sure you know all that.

WOMAN. No, I don't know all that.

AUNTIE AH. Oh she was wild about this other fella who let her down badly. I never heard the why's and how's of it but I know it nearly killed her. She only married your father because he asked her. Well, she wasn't the first and won't be the last.

WOMAN. And who was he? The one she was wild about?

AUNTIE AH. Never mind. That's as much as I'm telling.

WOMAN. So there's more to tell.

AUNTIE AH. Oh there is, there is, indeed there's more to tell.

WOMAN. Then don't withhold from me now.

AUNTIE AH. You have parcelled yourself from me your whole life and now you want information.

WOMAN. Don't make me beg … I'm on my deathbed.

AUNTIE AH. And that excuses everything?

WOMAN. You're a vicious old woman. It's not your information to keep.

AUNTIE AH. Oh, but it is.

WOMAN. May you choke on it.

AUNTIE AH. And me all the time thinking I'd nothing you wanted.

WOMAN. It would mean the world to me.

AUNTIE AH. And what was I? Your servant? No … we're quits now. Nurse my scald, girl, as I've nursed yours. *(And exit Auntie Ah.)*

SCARECROW. She was saving that. Poison, always poison. Since you were knee-high, cups of poison. I can tell you about her if you want.

WOMAN. You remember her?

SCARECROW. I remember her.

WOMAN. All this time you said nothing.

SCARECROW. You never asked me, you never asked enough of me at all.

WOMAN. I'm asking now.

SCARECROW. Well, first of all there's no mystery about her. The only heroic thing she did was die young.

WOMAN. Your cruelty has no bounds.

SCARECROW. What have I said?

WOMAN. I want to know how she drank her tea and you're rattling on about heroism. Christ, all I'm asking you is to tell me how she lived.

SCARECROW. Okay. She lived bitterly. I remember her battering the spuds into a venomous pulp for the dinner. I remember her vagueness on the beach, her refusal to play. I remember the weeping in darkened rooms, her obsession with Mass and fawning over the priest. I remember her belief that she was inferior and her living out of that belief with such conviction, such passion, such energy she invested in taking second place. All of which you have inherited. And underneath it all I remember this volcanic rage that erupted given any opportunity on the small, the weak, the helpless. Hardship was all she knew. Hardship was all she understood, hardship was her prayer in the morning and her evening song. A woman of rock, carved out of the rocks around her. Immovable. Devastating to behold from the cradle.

WOMAN. That wasn't her at all.

SCARECROW. Why would I lie? I loved her too.

WOMAN. So is that where my coldness comes from?

SCARECROW. Your conservatism, your inability to function either the right or the wrong side of the sheets.

WOMAN. All of that.

SCARECROW. You never knew there are two doors in and out of every house. Always to insist on the correct one, the narrow one, the one that has led you here. I'd like to write that letter now, before we run out of time.

WOMAN. There'll be no letter.

SCARECROW. You owe it to yourself.

WOMAN. No. Leave him be.

SCARECROW. Someone has to tell him he can't wreak havoc in people's lives the way he has done with yours.

WOMAN. You're smothering with revenge.

SCARECROW. Yes I am. If I was you, I'd have killed him long ago. You still think this man is worth dying for?

WOMAN. I'm not answering that question. Don't keep asking me that question.

SCARECROW. Well I've got news for you. You're not dying for him. You're leaving this planet because I have given up.

WOMAN. So if you decided we could live?

SCARECROW. But I have decided. Look, I'll see you out, that's more than most of my kind does, I'll see you to the last breath but only if you write that letter.

WOMAN. And if I don't?

SCARECROW. I'll walk away now.

WOMAN. *(Looks at Scarecrow a long time.)* Okay … I'll write the letter.

SCARECROW. And you'll take dictation from me?

WOMAN. Do I have a choice? *(Scarecrow gives her pen and paper. Woman starts writing.)*

SCARECROW. What are you doing? *(Takes paper. Reads.)* My darling, it's late and there are a few things I want to say to you. Well, for starters, cut out "darling."

WOMAN. What's wrong with "darling?"

SCARECROW. Just cross it out. It's late and there are things that must be said.

WOMAN. *(Writing.)* So hard … First I want to give instructions about my funeral.

SCARECROW. You can do that on a separate sheet after.

WOMAN. No, we'll do it first or he mightn't read it after your diatribe.

SCARECROW. He'll read it. As long as it's all about him, he'll read it. The ego of the man is unbelievable.

WOMAN. Will I write that down?

SCARECROW. Okay, do your funeral first.

WOMAN. *(Writing.)* The funeral. I'll underline it so he doesn't forget.

SCARECROW. You think he might forget to bury you?

WOMAN. I've already spoken to you about the baby's coffin. It will have disintegrated but tell the gravediggers what's left of it is to be placed on top of mine. Eventually he will sink back into me and maybe in time one glorious asphodel will spring from the manure of our bones. Don't forget to do this now. And don't carry me through the village in my coffin. I am not a hurler. Just from the hearse, which should be opposite the church door. If possible, hire four black horses with the black plumes. I know these are expensive and Demis Roussos playing as I'm carried up the aisle. "My Friend the Wind" or "Ever and Ever." I like both. Let my sons carry me as once I carried them. Get someone else to say the Mass, not Father Gant, he has no way with words.

SCARECROW. Okay, are you done?

WOMAN. Funeral clothes. *(Underlines it.)* On a hanger on my side of the wardrobe are the clothes I want to wear. My black velvet dress with the V neckline. My silk slip, my grey tights and my new black high heels, the ones I meant to wear for Christmas Day. They're in a box under the dress.

SCARECROW. Do corpses wear shoes?

WOMAN. *(Writing.)* Around my shoulders put the green lace cape. Don't join my hands and no rosary beads. It's too smug. Just put my arms out straight with my palms facing upwards. Leave my hair down and a trace of lipstick. No other makeup. Read these instructions to whoever lays me out. No prayer books, no holy medals, no scapulars. I suppose it would be too much to ask to put me in a *currach* and just float me on the tide. No, I'll cross that out, he'd never get it together. What else? Oh yeah, kissing. I don't want anyone kissing me except the children and yourself if you care to. I have a horror of being kissed when dead. I will taste of iron. My lips will be frozen. It will repel everyone. Better they just have a look and move on. And don't leave me in the church overnight. I never liked churches at night. Driving by them in the dark, I've always felt some fierce battle was taking place in there. I don't want to be in the middle of it. Don't leave me in the church overnight. I'll underline that three times. And a few exclamation marks. If you have ever felt anything for me, don't leave me in the church overnight.

SCARECROW. Right, the purpose of this letter. New paragraph.

WOMAN. Just a sec. *(Writing furiously.)*

SCARECROW. If you'd put as much thought into your life.

WOMAN. I'm just telling him to get everyone drunk after the funeral. I've always loved funerals, especially the afters, the excitement, the food, the drink, the relief on everyone's face. Not even the best behaved can hide their glee, there's something in us that loves the harmony of seeing someone out. The pure animal delight, as if every cell in our bodies is shrieking, it wasn't me, it wasn't me.

Drink up, dance, flirt, tell them to have sex on my grave. Have trays of champagne and mulled wine, pass them across the flowers and the wreaths. Fall over me. I'll be listening, I'll be having my own spectral glass beneath.

SCARECROW. Are you through?

WOMAN. Yes, I'm through. It's your turn now. Now we're going to get a lecture on the meaning of life. Go on, do your worst, you seething superior sow. *(Begins writing.)*

SCARECROW. I haven't said anything yet.

WOMAN. *(Writing.)* I'm just putting a disclaimer before this bit. This is not me but the other one, the filthy old scarecrow who has hounded me down the years. Okay, shoot.

SCARECROW. On the brink of extinction I have a few things to say.

WOMAN. *(Mockingly.)* On the brink of extinction …

SCARECROW. Heading into the dark, I want to leave a trail of darkness after me. I want you to wake at three in the morning with frost on the window pane on some starless and moonless night. I want you to think of me packed into the hard cold clay. And when you think of me down there I want you to remember you have killed me as surely as if you had taken an ice pick and plunged it to the hilt.

WOMAN. I got sick. I died. That's all there is to it.

SCARECROW. And what about me?

WOMAN. You can't lay all this at his door.

SCARECROW. Just write it down. I want to talk about your cowardice. Write it down. I want to talk about your parsimony. I said write it down. I want to talk about what you have withheld from me and from your children. Let's start with your cowardice. Before the second child was born you had left. Question? Then why didn't you stay gone? Why all the returns? Why all the whingeing and the whining confessions and promises of change? Why all the ridiculous attempts to appear complicated? I never hated you more than when you'd return after another sleazy transgression. Leave out the brazen lies of it. Leave out my heart in shreds, even leave out the children for a minute. Leave all of that out and consider for one moment what you have done to yourself. You are without pride, without dignity, without any sense of who you are or of where your place is in this world or what you are here for.

WOMAN. And you know what I'm here for?

SCARECROW. Don't interrupt me! You have reeled through my life wreaking havoc at every turn. Well, I for one am crying out at last. Enough. You will go no further with me. I want you to know I am going to my grave with my heart broken, yes, but not for you. My heart broken for myself and my children that I allowed your puling, whining need ensnare me so.

WOMAN. *(Softly.)* Yes.

SCARECROW. And finally I want to talk to you about what we were and what we have become.

WOMAN. What have the years done to us? Where did we go to when we weren't looking?

SCARECROW. It was the first betrayal. The ones after were nothing compared with the first.

WOMAN. Yes, the others I've become cynical about as if they happened to someone else. I even tried to play you at your own game for a while, which only took me further from myself. You told me I was the one, the only one and I believed you.

WOMAN and SCARECROW And thought it would be so for all of time apportioned to us here. And then you denied me. And how. For a very long time I thought I had done something. And then I believed you had just stopped loving me. I realise now I was mistaken in my generous estimation of your capacity to love, for it is clear as day that you are and have always been and I presume will continue to be incapable of loving anyone, that is, anyone except yourself and your insatiable ego. And what drives my hatred now is my blindness to what you have slowly taken from me down the years, that is, my capacity to love which was boundless in the beginning, long ago when we walked by the river. Be aware I go to my grave bewildered by your cruelty, I go angry, I go unforgiving and I wonder now when the time comes how you will go to yours. *(Pause.)*

WOMAN. Look after the children, my unwanted gifts to you, my consolation prizes to myself.

SCARECROW. Put it somewhere he'll find it. *(Woman does. Enter Him.)*

WOMAN. Tell Auntie Ah to leave this house.

HIM. What has she done now?

WOMAN. She's not to lay me out. I dreamt she did something to my stomach with a sort of revolving cheese knife. I don't want her near me again. Dead or alive.

HIM. I'll put a bounty on her head.

WOMAN. I'm serious.

HIM. I won't let her near you.

WOMAN. HAs the post come?

HIM. Yes.

WOMAN. Anything for me? Anything interesting?

HIM. What are you waiting for? A love letter?

WOMAN. I wouldn't say no to a love letter right now.

HIM. Your Visa bill came.

WOMAN. My Visa bill has always interested you.

HIM. Nearly two grand in a shoe shop.

WOMAN. Imagine, a Visa bill ago, I was flinging credit cards at shop assistants.

HIM. Where are all the shoes? Can I bring them back?

WOMAN. No, you can't.

HIM. So who's going to pay for them?

WOMAN. I enjoyed buying those shoes. There was a pair of crocodile skin boots, mad heels, real don't-mess-with-me boots.

HIM. On your deathbed and still talking about material possessions, rattling on about shoes.

WOMAN. And what should I be rattling on about? You think I should be calm and resigned and philosophical. You think the dying mull over eternity. They don't. They don't. They think about shoes and how they'll never get a chance to wear them. And when I land in eternity I'll still be praising those boots. I'll describe them to Him 'til He aches to have a human foot the size of mine that He can encase in crocodile-skin boots. If I had another fifty years I'd put them on every day. I'd wear them to bed. You savage! How dare you accost me with Visa bills as I draw my last breath!

HIM. Well, forgive me if I mention a small detail. There are eight children to be fed and dressed and educated.

WOMAN. That detail never bothered you until now. And if I know you as well as I do, you won't feed or educate them if you can get away with it. I'm leaving orphans. Orphans! You'll begrudge them a bowl of Weetabix. God help them with you at the helm. Forever turning off the hot water and the lights and the heat. Tell me what it is you hate about heat and light. What is it about hot water that drives you crazy? I dreamt last night you were locking up potatoes. Yes, I said to myself, that's it, I married a man who locks up potatoes. Christ, get me out of here quick. You'll have my pension, my life insurance. I won't cost you a penny. Here, I'll even pay for my own funeral. *(Rips open envelope from Auntie Ah, flings wads of money around.)*

HIM. I'll pay for your funeral.

WOMAN. You don't deserve to pay for my funeral. Take it. Auntie Ah gave it to me.

HIM. We don't need Auntie Ah's charity. I'll give it back to her.

WOMAN. Why are you here? What is you want? I have nothing left to give.

HIM. Do you want me to go?

WOMAN. Don't you have a date?

HIM. No, I don't.

WOMAN. You cancelled. You'll see her at the weekend.

HIM. This is the weekend.

WOMAN. Are you looking forward to your freedom?

HIM. Are you looking forward to yours?

WOMAN. I'm going to have a very long sleep. I'm looking forward to that. I haven't slept a night since I met you.

HIM. Another blot on my copybook.

WOMAN. And you have fantasised about my death.

HIM. I have not.

WOMAN. I know a little about fantasies of escape. I wasn't born yesterday.

HIM. I thought to relegate you to the background. That's all … my most vicious daydreams assumed you'd be living, healthy, and if not happy, then at least bearing up … but living … always living … you have no right to leave me like this. *(He is close to tears. Woman looks at him standing there.)* Take your fill of me. I am guilty, yes … I have no defence. Whatever you think I have done to you I have done and worse but, Christ, don't leave me like this.

WOMAN. I'm sorry … I didn't mean to … come and lie beside me … come under the covers … *(He gets into bed beside her. He wraps himself around her.)*

HIM. Am I hurting you?

WOMAN. No … I've missed you in bed beside me.

HIM. I've missed you too.

WOMAN. Ah, old friend … Old battle-weary foe.

HIM. Is that what I am?

WOMAN. I think so.

HIM. Your feet are cold.

WOMAN. Is it snowing?

HIM. Yes. Would you like to look out the window?

WOMAN. How much snow? Inches?

HIM. More.

WOMAN. What does it mean if I go with the snow?

HIM. If you have to go, winter is the time.

WOMAN. What do you mean?

HIM. You're following the seasons.

WOMAN. I was born in winter too. The symmetry is appalling and I remember something else about snow. A woman gave me a lift once because it was snowing. We drove and drove through all that whiteness until finally she pulled in at the courtyard of an old house with a wooden balcony going round it. And on the wooden balcony painted scenes in that old red and gold. we sit looking at these painted scenes, the snow whirling, the trees, the road, the courtyard, and then Christ passes by in a cart. He's a painting and not a painting, and the woman and I stare, transfixed as he glides past, quizzical, peaceful. And his passing is such we don't want to share it, speak of it, we refuse to look at one another, refuse to acknowledge what we have just seen, are seeing in the snow in that courtyard.

HIM. When was this?

WOMAN. I don't think it has happened yet. Are you drinking these days? These nights?

HIM. Like a fish.

WOMAN. Good. The wine will see you through.

HIM. I'll go off it soon ... Did you really have lovers?

WOMAN. Yes, I did.

HIM. So sly.

WOMAN. Does it bother you?

HIM. Yes, it bothers me ... Why did you wait 'til the end to tell me?

WOMAN. I think because it never occurred to you to ask.

HIM. So what was the last three decades about?

WOMAN. You and I? It was exile, of course. Exile from the best of ourselves ... Beasts in a cave with night coming on ... no way to live at all.

HIM. You have some nerve. The one thing I was always sure of ... thought I was sure of was you. You there no matter what ... you there for me and me only.

WOMAN. For a long time I was.

HIM. How long?

WOMAN. Too long.

HIM. I want dates.

WOMAN. Leave out the prose. It's enough to realise we were nothing but a façade for procreation.

HIM. No, I want to know when you turned. I want to know how many. Who? Do I know them?

WOMAN. Grim conquests, most of them.

HIM. Most of them.

WOMAN. There was one I almost … He gave me this. *(He takes diamond ring off her finger, looks at it. Takes wedding and engagement rings from his pocket and puts them back on her finger.)*

HIM. You will wear my rings to your grave.

WOMAN. The rings go to the girls.

HIM. The rings go where I say they go.

WOMAN. Not this time. *(Takes them off.)*

HIM. *(Takes them from her.)* I'll put them on when you're dead.

WOMAN. You do and I'll put a curse on you.

HIM. You already have. My whole life with you has been one long vicious curse. If I have to solder them to your fingers you'll wear these rings to your grave. You think to escape me now at the end, to slip away having spewed the devious details of your life all over me. My life was meant to be various. Huge.

WOMAN. And mine?

HIM. Yours is over. It's over and I'm meant to pick up after you. The mess you're leaving me with. And to top it all, it was just a game, a game of charades for you. All the time deceiving me.

WOMAN. So subterfuge is your domain?

HIM. Yes. Mine. Women are not allowed that. The whole point of a woman is not so much wanting her, that waxes and wanes, but that no one else can go near her.

WOMAN. There have been a few small advances since that Neanderthal theory first did the rounds.

HIM. Like hell, there have. You know our wedding day was the end of the whole thing.

WOMAN. Yes, most marry at the end. Yes, our wedding was the last door closing. The click has taken us until now to hear. Well, we were always slow learners. Each child a blind hope for what?

HIM. What have they got to do with anything? They're just there. Strangers. I have problems remembering their names.

WOMAN. You seem very proud of that fact. Well, they'll survive you whether you remember their names or not, as I survived my parents or lack of, as you survived yours. We don't really figure except as gargoyles to bitch about to their lovers. They'll have the last word on you as you'll have the last word on me. If you dare make a sentimental speech at my funeral, I'll rise up out of the coffin and rip your tongue out.

HIM. I'll herd you to your grave like a cow to a byre.

WOMAN. You'll come up with some whinging panegyric, I know you.

HIM. You know nothing.

WOMAN. Could you put me in the car and we drive out west? See the Atlantic. I'd like to finish up back west.

HIM. You can't be moved.

WOMAN. You want to be near her.

HIM. And if I do?

WOMAN. I want to drive west. I need expanse now, the open sea, the wolfish mountains. That's what's been missing. Don't let me die here.

HIM. I can't. The snow. The doctors said ... It was a huge achievement to get you home.

WOMAN. You've been talking to her.

HIM. Yes. Briefly.

WOMAN. And what did you talk about briefly?

HIM. We talked about you.

WOMAN. How my death is coming on. Will she never go? You said that to her.

HIM. I said no such thing.

WOMAN. I heard you whispering on the phone to her last night. I heard you in the hall.

HIM. Yes, she rang last night. I asked her not to call the house.

WOMAN. So virtuous. So honest. So truth-loving. What a lucky girl I am.

HIM. She wanted me to tell you something.

WOMAN. There's nothing she can tell me.

HIM. She just asked me to tell you.

WOMAN. I don't want to hear it.

HIM. Just that she's sorry for the way she treated you that night you turned up in the rain.

WOMAN. I refuse to discuss her.

HIM. That's why she rang. She can't sleep over you. She has never behaved like that with anyone before.

WOMAN. And you believe her. You have no taste, no judgement. How can you stay with a woman who treats your wife with such contempt? How can you bear to be around someone who looks on her fellow creatures with such unbridled scorn?

HIM. You've had your scornful moments too.

WOMAN. No, I have not. I have raged, howled, wheedled, blundered, but I have not scorned. My abiding feeling for my fellow journeyers has been one of pity, yes, pity and a gushing unasked-for love. Misguided, I know, but genuine. And never scorn. Maybe scorn would've kept me alive ... But why do we always end up talking about her? She's ugly, she's boring, she doesn't even have the redeeming vice of witchery. She's a hag without the warts. If it's a hag you want, there are uglier and more dangerous around. Or if it's my jealousy you crave, then pick someone worthy of my jealousy. And keep her away from my children.

HIM. She has no interest in your children.

WOMAN. Will you talk to them about me from time to time?

HIM. Yes of course I will.

WOMAN. Try to keep me alive for them, for lately I have begun to suspect if there is such a thing as eternity, it resides in the hearts and minds of those who have loved us. For time, memory, eternity are merely inventions of the fallen world. And it is here among the fallen we will be remembered and forgotten.

SCARECROW. Then what do you call that thing in the wardrobe?

WOMAN. That thing with the cobalt beak. That thing is the opposite of eternity.

SCARECROW. Then what am I?

HIM. What is it, my dear?

WOMAN. I'm talking to Scarecrow. What are you? I'll tell you what you are. You are the parasite who has thwarted my every joy. Without you, I would've been happy with him. Without you, I would've wanted nothing.

SCARECROW. Well, if that's how you feel I can go right now.

WOMAN. Then go! Go! Go! I'm sick of your threats.

SCARECROW. And leave you with him?

WOMAN. Yes, leave me with him.

SCARECROW. There was another way to live.

WOMAN. Yes, there was and I didn't find it.

SCARECROW. You didn't even look. *(And exit Scarecrow.)*

HIM. Your feet are ice.

WOMAN. Then it must be nearly over.

HIM. Will I bring in the children?

WOMAN. They're gone … They're gone … They're mostly gone.

HIM. It's alright … It's alright … Is there anything …

WOMAN. Scarecrow … go after Scarecrow … bring her back.

HIM. Some champagne … you said once you'd like to drink champagne at the end.

WOMAN. Did I?

HIM. I have a bottle in the fridge.

WOMAN. Am I capable of a glass, do you think?

HIM. Yes, let's have chapagne.

WOMAN. And bring the dish-glasses … not the fluted.

HIM. Where would they be?

HIM. I'll find them … Wait now … wait easy … I'll be back in a sec. *(And exit Him. Woman lies there. Hold a minute. Wardrobe door creaks open. Enter Death from the wardrobe, regal, terrifying, one black wing, clawed feet, taloned fingers. Stands looking at Woman, shakes itself down. Woman stares at him.)*

WOMAN. *(Calls weakly.)* Scarecrow … I'm begging you … he's here … I can't do this on my own.

SCARECROW. You don't have to, dear.

WOMAN. Scarecrow … is that you … but I thought …

SCARECROW. That I was your slave … that you were in charge? Not so. Not so. I've a few forms to fill out, so just bear with me for a second. *(Plucks a feather from her wing. Takes out parchment, unrolls it.)* So you're nearly there? Exciting, isn't it?

WOMAN. You swore you'd see me out.

SCARECROW. And I will. Now I need ink. *(Scarecrow takes Woman's hhand, pierces her wrist; a fountain of blood shoots out. Scarecrow dips the quill into Woman's wrist. A cry of pain from Woman.)* I know, my chicken, I know, it is never easy becoming the past tense. Okay, you said you had brains to burn?

WOMAN. Then I must habve burnt them. *(Scarecrow writes, dipping the quill in and out of Woman's wrist.)* Scarecrow, don't do this to me.

SCARECROW. I have no choice. You think I want to do this? It's out of my control. *(Reads.)* Next question. Why did you stop seeking?

WOMAN. That's the big one, isn't it?

SCARECROW. No time now except for the big ones. *(Waits with quill poised.)* You'll answer the question, please. The paperwork must be in order.

WOMAN. Why did I stop seeking? … I didn't know what to look for and I was afraid what I would find.

SCARECROW. *(Writing.)* Yeah, that's the usual excuse we get. And love? Why did you not flee when love had flown?

WOMAN. But it hasn't flown.

SCARECROW. It says here it has flown.

WOMAN. It hasn't. He's here.

SCARECROW. Where?

WOMAN. He's getting me champagne. Anyway, how could I leave my children?

SCARECROW. You're leaving them now.

WOMAN. That's a different leaving.

SCARECROW. It certainly is. We're not talking a few years here. We're talking never. Never. We're talking the five nevers and the four howls.

WOMAN. So are you saying I could have turned up at the lover's door with the eight of them.

SCARECROW. I'm saying exactly that.

WOMAN. With what? How? For starters is would have taken two car journeys. I would've had to arrive twice. And to arrive twice at the lover's door is worse than not arriving at all. Give me credit for some timing. These are stupid questions. Who designed this questionnaire?

SCARECROW. You did.

WOMAN. Will all of this be used against me?

SCARECROW. It will be used. *(Reads.)* And the children, admit it, they were your shield to beat the world away?

WOMAN. Yes, they were.

SCARECROW. *(Reads.)* You hid behind the nappies and the bottles.

WOMAN. The mountainous bellies and the cut knees, the broken arms, the temperatures, the school uniforms, the football, the music. Yes, I hid behind it all. Yes, I used them. They were my little soldiers. I was the fortress. And how they protected me from terrors imagined and terrors real, my soothers, my buffers to fortune. And I'm sure I've damaged them in some vital irreparable way, but I have also loved them with a hopeless, enchanted love.

SCARECROW. (Dipping the quill into Woman's wrist.) This well is dry. I'm sorry, I have to do this. *(Pierces Woman's neck. A fountain*

of blood, small, from Woman.)
WOMAN. Scarecrow, don't ... please don't.
SCARECROW. We can't go back now. *(Reads.)* And if you could take a thought with you, what would it be?
WOMAN. What would it be ... that I have never felt at home here.
SCARECROW. *(Writing.)* Very few do.
WOMAN. We don't belong here. There must be another Earth. And yet there was a moment when I thought it might be possible here. A moment so elusive it's hardly worth mentioning. An ordinary day with the ordinary sun of a late Indian summer shining on the grass as I sat in the car waiting to collect the children from school. Rusalka on the radio, her song to the moon. They say it's an unlucky song. *(Fade in "Song to the Moon" from the opera* Rusalka.*)* Rusalka pouring her heart out to the moon, her love for the mortal, make me human, she sings, make me human so I can have him. And something about the alignment of sun and wind and song on this most ordinary of afternoons stays with me, though what it means is beyond me and what I felt is forgotten now, but the bare facts, me, the sun, the shivering grass, the trees, Rusalka singing to the moon. And I wonder, is this not the prayer each of us whispers when we pause to consider. Make me human. Make me human. And then divine. And I wonder is it for these elusive prayers we are here, these half sentences that vanish into the ether almost before we can utter them. Living is almost nothing and we brave little mortals investing so much in it.
SCARECROW. You're determined to go with romance on your lips.
WOMAN. I know as well as the next that the arc of our time here bends to tragedy. How can it be otherwise when we think where we're going? But we must mark those moments, those passionate moments, however small. I looked up passionate in the dictionary once because I thought I had never known it. And do you know what passion means?
SCARECROW. Yes. It comes from the Latin, *patior,* to suffer.
WOMAN. Well, I said to myself, if that's the definition of passion, then I have known passion. More. I have lived a passionate life. Yes, I have lived passionately unbeknownst to myself. Here it lay on my doorstep and I all the time looking out for it. (Scarecrow finishes writing, rolls up the parchment. Puts it into a bag of scrools hanging from her waist.)
SCARECROW. That's out of the way ... I'm afraid it's time.

WOMAN. But I'm not ready.

SCARECROW. It's time to go.

WOMAN. Scarecrow, please …my children …

SCARECROW. I know, I know, but don't fight me … you won't win this time.

WOMAN. Just hold on 'til he comes back.

SCARECROW. You want him to watch you die.

WOMAN. He was the closest I came to the thing itself … I think I've stopped breathing.

SCARECROW. Yes, it's over.

WOMAN. *(Throws herself on Scarecrow.)* Oh, Scarecrow … the next breath isn't coming.

SCARECROW. And won't ever. *(And she dies in Scarecrow's arms. Hold a minute and fade lights and music.)*

End of Play

PROPERTY LIST

CD
Hand mirror
Medicine, beaker
Bottle of wine, corkscrew, glasses
Diamond ring
Envelope of money
Clump of black feathers
Rosary beads
Pen and paper
Bottle of champagne, two glasses

SOUND EFFECTS

Song on CD player
Piano music
Opera music

NEW PLAYS

★ **YELLOW FACE by David Henry Hwang.** Asian-American playwright DHH leads a protest against the casting of Jonathan Pryce as the Eurasian pimp in the original Broadway production of *Miss Saigon*, condemning the practice as "yellowface." The lines between truth and fiction blur with hilarious and moving results in this unreliable memoir. "A pungent play of ideas with a big heart." *–Variety.* "Fabulously inventive." *–The New Yorker.* [5M, 2W] ISBN: 978-0-8222-2301-6

★ **33 VARIATIONS by Moisés Kaufmann.** A mother coming to terms with her daughter. A composer coming to terms with his genius. And, even though they're separated by 200 years, these two people share an obsession that might, even just for a moment, make time stand still. "A compellingly original and thoroughly watchable play for today." *–Talkin' Broadway.* [4M, 4W] ISBN: 978-0-8222-2392-4

★ **BOOM by Peter Sinn Nachtrieb.** A grad student's online personal ad lures a mysterious journalism student to his subterranean research lab. But when a major catastrophic event strikes the planet, their date takes on evolutionary significance and the fate of humanity hangs in the balance. "Darkly funny dialogue." *–NY Times.* "Literate, coarse, thoughtful, sweet, scabrously inappropriate." *–Washington City Paper.* [1M, 2W] ISBN: 978-0-8222-2370-2

★ **LOVE, LOSS AND WHAT I WORE by Nora Ephron and Delia Ephron, based on the book by Ilene Beckerman.** A play of monologues and ensemble pieces about women, clothes and memory covering all the important subjects—mothers, prom dresses, mothers, buying bras, mothers, hating purses and why we only wear black. "Funny, compelling." *–NY Times.* "So funny and so powerful." *–WowOwow.com.* [5W] ISBN: 978-0-8222-2355-9

★ **CIRCLE MIRROR TRANSFORMATION by Annie Baker.** When four lost New Englanders enrolled in Marty's community center drama class experiment with harmless games, hearts are quietly torn apart, and tiny wars of epic proportions are waged and won. "Absorbing, unblinking and sharply funny." *–NY Times.* [2M, 3W] ISBN: 978-0-8222-2445-7

★ **BROKE-OLOGY by Nathan Louis Jackson.** The King family has weathered the hardships of life and survived with their love for each other intact. But when two brothers are called home to take care of their father, they find themselves strangely at odds. "Engaging dialogue." *–TheaterMania.com.* "Assured, bighearted." *–Time Out.* [3M, 1W] ISBN: 978-0-8222-2428-0

DRAMATISTS PLAY SERVICE, INC.
440 Park Avenue South, New York, NY 10016 212-683-8960 Fax 212-213-1539
postmaster@dramatists.com www.dramatists.com

NEW PLAYS

★ **A CIVIL WAR CHRISTMAS: AN AMERICAN MUSICAL CELEBRATION by Paula Vogel, music by Daryl Waters.** It's 1864, and Washington, D.C. is settling down to the coldest Christmas Eve in years. Intertwining many lives, this musical shows us that the gladness of one's heart is the best gift of all. "Boldly inventive theater, warm and affecting." –*Talkin' Broadway.* "Crisp strokes of dialogue." –*NY Times.* [12M, 5W] ISBN: 978-0-8222-2361-0

★ **SPEECH & DEBATE by Stephen Karam.** Three teenage misfits in Salem, Oregon discover they are linked by a sex scandal that's rocked their town. "Savvy comedy." –*Variety.* "Hilarious, cliché-free, and immensely entertaining." –*NY Times.* "A strong, rangy play." –*NY Newsday.* [2M, 2W] ISBN: 978-0-8222-2286-6

★ **DIVIDING THE ESTATE by Horton Foote.** Matriarch Stella Gordon is determined not to divide her 100-year-old Texas estate, despite her family's declining wealth and the looming financial crisis. But her three children have another plan. "Goes for laughs and succeeds." –*NY Daily News.* "The theatrical equivalent of a page-turner." –*Bloomberg.com.* [4M, 9W] ISBN: 978-0-8222-2398-6

★ **WHY TORTURE IS WRONG, AND THE PEOPLE WHO LOVE THEM by Christopher Durang.** Christopher Durang turns political humor upside down with this raucous and provocative satire about America's growing homeland "insecurity." "A smashing new play." –*NY Observer.* "You may laugh yourself silly." –*Bloomberg News.* [4M, 3W] ISBN: 978-0-8222-2401-3

★ **FIFTY WORDS by Michael Weller.** While their nine-year-old son is away for the night on his first sleepover, Adam and Jan have an evening alone together, beginning a suspenseful nightlong roller-coaster ride of revelation, rancor, passion and humor. "Mr. Weller is a bold and productive dramatist." –*NY Times.* [1M, 1W] ISBN: 978-0-8222-2348-1

★ **BECKY'S NEW CAR by Steven Dietz.** Becky Foster is caught in middle age, middle management and in a middling marriage—with no prospects for change on the horizon. Then one night a socially inept and grief-struck millionaire stumbles into the car dealership where Becky works. "Gently and consistently funny." –*Variety.* "Perfect blend of hilarious comedy and substantial weight." –*Broadway Hour.* [4M, 3W] ISBN: 978-0-8222-2393-1

DRAMATISTS PLAY SERVICE, INC.
440 Park Avenue South, New York, NY 10016 212-683-8960 Fax 212-213-1539
postmaster@dramatists.com www.dramatists.com

NEW PLAYS

★ **AT HOME AT THE ZOO by Edward Albee.** Edward Albee delves deeper into his play THE ZOO STORY by adding a first act, HOMELIFE, which precedes Peter's fateful meeting with Jerry on a park bench in Central Park. "An essential and heartening experience." *–NY Times.* "Darkly comic and thrilling." *–Time Out.* "Genuinely fascinating." *–Journal News.* [2M, 1W] ISBN: 978-0-8222-2317-7

★ **PASSING STRANGE book and lyrics by Stew, music by Stew and Heidi Rodewald, created in collaboration with Annie Dorsen.** A daring musical about a young bohemian that takes you from black middle-class America to Amsterdam, Berlin and beyond on a journey towards personal and artistic authenticity. "Fresh, exuberant, bracingly inventive, bitingly funny, and full of heart." *–NY Times.* "The freshest musical in town!" *–Wall Street Journal.* "Excellent songs and a vulnerable heart." *–Variety.* [4M, 3W] ISBN: 978-0-8222-2400-6

★ **REASONS TO BE PRETTY by Neil LaBute.** Greg really, truly adores his girlfriend, Steph. Unfortunately, he also thinks she has a few physical imperfections, and when he mentions them, all hell breaks loose. "Tight, tense and emotionally true." *–Time Magazine.* "Lively and compulsively watchable." *–The Record.* [2M, 2W] ISBN: 978-0-8222-2394-8

★ **OPUS by Michael Hollinger.** With only a few days to rehearse a grueling Beethoven masterpiece, a world-class string quartet struggles to prepare their highest-profile performance ever—a televised ceremony at the White House. "Intimate, intense and profoundly moving." *–Time Out.* "Worthy of scores of bravissimos." *–BroadwayWorld.com.* [4M, 1W] ISBN: 978-0-8222-2363-4

★ **BECKY SHAW by Gina Gionfriddo.** When an evening calculated to bring happiness takes a dark turn, crisis and comedy ensue in this wickedly funny play that asks what we owe the people we love and the strangers who land on our doorstep. "As engrossing as it is ferociously funny." *–NY Times.* "Gionfriddo is some kind of genius." *–Variety.* [2M, 3W] ISBN: 978-0-8222-2402-0

★ **KICKING A DEAD HORSE by Sam Shepard.** Hobart Struther's horse has just dropped dead. In an eighty-minute monologue, he discusses what path brought him here in the first place, the fate of his marriage, his career, politics and eventually the nature of the universe. "Deeply instinctual and intuitive." *–NY Times.* "The brilliance is in the infinite reverberations Shepard extracts from his simple metaphor." *–TheaterMania.* [1M, 1W] ISBN: 978-0-8222-2336-8

DRAMATISTS PLAY SERVICE, INC.
440 Park Avenue South, New York, NY 10016 212-683-8960 Fax 212-213-1539
postmaster@dramatists.com www.dramatists.com

NEW PLAYS

★ **AUGUST: OSAGE COUNTY by Tracy Letts.** WINNER OF THE 2008 PULITZER PRIZE AND TONY AWARD. When the large Weston family reunites after Dad disappears, their Oklahoma homestead explodes in a maelstrom of repressed truths and unsettling secrets. "Fiercely funny and bitingly sad." *–NY Times.* "Ferociously entertaining." *–Variety.* "A hugely ambitious, highly combustible saga." *–NY Daily News.* [6M, 7W] ISBN: 978-0-8222-2300-9

★ **RUINED by Lynn Nottage.** WINNER OF THE 2009 PULITZER PRIZE. Set in a small mining town in Democratic Republic of Congo, RUINED is a haunting, probing work about the resilience of the human spirit during times of war. "A full-immersion drama of shocking complexity and moral ambiguity." *–Variety.* "Sincere, passionate, courageous." *–Chicago Tribune.* [8M, 4W] ISBN: 978-0-8222-2390-0

★ **GOD OF CARNAGE by Yasmina Reza, translated by Christopher Hampton.** WINNER OF THE 2009 TONY AWARD. A playground altercation between boys brings together their Brooklyn parents, leaving the couples in tatters as the rum flows and tensions explode. "Satisfyingly primitive entertainment." *–NY Times.* "Elegant, acerbic, entertainingly fueled on pure bile." *–Variety.* [2M, 2W] ISBN: 978-0-8222-2399-3

★ **THE SEAFARER by Conor McPherson.** Sharky has returned to Dublin to look after his irascible, aging brother. Old drinking buddies Ivan and Nicky are holed up at the house too, hoping to play some cards. But with the arrival of a stranger from the distant past, the stakes are raised ever higher. "Dark and enthralling Christmas fable." *–NY Times.* "A timeless classic." *–Hollywood Reporter.* [5M] ISBN: 978-0-8222-2284-2

★ **THE NEW CENTURY by Paul Rudnick.** When the playwright is Paul Rudnick, expectations are geared for a play both hilarious and smart, and this provocative and outrageous comedy is no exception. "The one-liners fly like rockets." *–NY Times.* "The funniest playwright around." *–Journal News.* [2M, 3W] ISBN: 978-0-8222-2315-3

★ **SHIPWRECKED! AN ENTERTAINMENT—THE AMAZING ADVENTURES OF LOUIS DE ROUGEMONT (AS TOLD BY HIMSELF) by Donald Margulies.** The amazing story of bravery, survival and celebrity that left nineteenth-century England spellbound. Dare to be whisked away. "A deft, literate narrative." *–LA Times.* "Springs to life like a theatrical pop-up book." *–NY Times.* [2M, 1W] ISBN: 978-0-8222-2341-2

DRAMATISTS PLAY SERVICE, INC.
440 Park Avenue South, New York, NY 10016 212-683-8960 Fax 212-213-1539
postmaster@dramatists.com   www.dramatists.com